DIARY 2025

2025 YEAR PLANNER

The year 2025 (MMXXV) is a non-leap year, it begins on a Wednesday.

JANUARY

M	T	W	T	F	S	S
		1	2	3	4	5
6	7	8	9	10	11	12
13	14	15	16	17	18	19
20	21	22	23	24	25	26
27	28	29	30	31		

FEBRUARY

M	T	W	T	F	S	S
					1	2
3	4	5	6	7	8	9
10	11	12	13	14	15	16
17	18	19	20	21	22	23
24	25	26	27	28		

MARCH

M	T	W	T	F	S	S
					1	2
3	4	5	6	7	8	9
10	11	12	13	14	15	16
17	18	19	20	21	22	23
24	25	26	27	28	29	30
31						

APRIL

M	T	W	T	F	S	S
	1	2	3	4	5	6
7	8	9	10	11	12	13
14	15	16	17	18	19	20
21	22	23	24	25	26	27
28	29	30				

MAY

M	T	W	T	F	S	S
		1	2	3	4	
5	6	7	8	9	10	11
12	13	14	15	16	17	18
19	20	21	22	23	24	25
26	27	28	29	30	31	

JUNE

M	T	W	T	F	S	S
						1
2	3	4	5	6	7	8
9	10	11	12	13	14	15
16	17	18	19	20	21	22
23	24	25	26	27	28	29
30						

JULY

M	T	W	T	F	S	S
	1	2	3	4	5	6
7	8	9	10	11	12	13
14	15	16	17	18	19	20
21	22	23	24	25	26	27
28	29	30	31			

AUGUST

M	T	W	T	F	S	S
				1	2	3
4	5	6	7	8	9	10
11	12	13	14	15	16	17
18	19	20	21	22	23	24
25	26	27	28	29	30	31

SEPTEMBER

M	T	W	T	F	S	S
1	2	3	4	5	6	7
8	9	10	11	12	13	14
15	16	17	18	19	20	21
22	23	24	25	26	27	28
29	30					

OCTOBER

M	T	W	T	F	S	S
		1	2	3	4	5
6	7	8	9	10	11	12
13	14	15	16	17	18	19
20	21	22	23	24	25	26
27	28	29	30	31		

NOVEMBER

M	T	W	T	F	S	S
					1	2
3	4	5	6	7	8	9
10	11	12	13	14	15	16
17	18	19	20	21	22	23
24	25	26	27	28	29	30

DECEMBER

M	T	W	T	F	S	S
1	2	3	4	5	6	7
8	9	10	11	12	13	14
15	16	17	18	19	20	21
22	23	24	25	26	27	28
29	30	31				

Did you know?

Between 13th September and the 21st – The 2025 World Athletics Championships will take place in Tokyo.

NAMES AND ADDRESSES

INTERNATIONAL DIALING CODES

Afghanistan	+93	Chad	+235
Albania	+355	Chile	+56
Algeria	+213	China	+86
Andorra	+376	Colombia	+57
Angola	+244	Comoros	+269
Argentina	+54	Cook Islands	+682
Armenia	+374	Costa Rica	+506
Aruba	+297	Côte D'Ivoire	+225
Australia	+61	Croatia	+385
Austria	+43	Cuba	+53
Azerbaijan	+994	Cyprus	+357
Bahamas	+1	Czech Rep	+420
Bahrain	+973	Denmark	+45
Bangladesh	+880	Djibouti	+253
Belarus	+375	Ecuador	+593
Belgium	+32	Egypt	+20
Belize	+501	Eritrea	+291
Benin	+229	Estonia	+372
Bhutan	+975	Ethiopia	+251
Bolivia	+591	Falklands	+500
Botswana	+267	Faroe Islands	+298
Brazil	+55	Fiji	+679
Bulgaria	+359	Finland	+358
Burundi	+257	France	+33
Cambodia	+855	Georgia	+995
Cameroon	+237	Germany	+49
Canada	+1	Ghana	+233
Cape Verde	+238	Gibraltar	+350

Greece	+30	Malaysia	+60
Greenland	+299	Malta	+356
Guatemala	+502	Mexico	+52
Guinea	+224	Monaco	+377
Guyana	+592	Nepal	+977
Haiti	+509	Netherlands	+31
Honduras	+504	New Zealand	+64
Hong Kong	+852	Nigeria	+234
Hungary	+36	Norway	+47
Iceland	+354	Pakistan	+92
India	+91	Panama	+507
Indonesia	+62	Paraguay	+595
Iran	+98	Peru	+51
Iraq	+964	Philippines	+63
Ireland	+353	Poland	+48
Israel	+972	Portugal	+351
Italy	+39	Qatar	+974
Japan	+81	Russia	+7
Kazakhstan	+7	Singapore	+65
Kenya	+254	South Africa	+27
Korea (N)	+850	Spain	+34
Korea (S)	+82	Sweden	+46
Kuwait	+965	Switzerland	+41
Kyrgyzstan	+996	Thailand	+66
Latvia	+371	Ukraine	+380
Lebanon	+961	UAE	+971
Libya	+218	UK	+44
Lithuania	+370	USA	+1
Luxembourg	+352	Uruguay	+598
Madagascar	+261	Zambia	+260

JANUARY 2025

Week 1

Did you know?
Starting on 8th of January - The 2025 World Men's Handball Championship will be held in Croatia, Denmark and Norway.

On 13th of January - The 2025 Winter World University Games will be held in Turin, Italy.

20th of Janaury - The winners of the 2025 United States presidential election are scheduled to be inaugurated as President and Vice President of the United States

Wednesday   1   *New Year's Day*

Thursday   2

Friday   3

Saturday   4

Sunday   5

JANUARY 2025

Week 2

Monday   6

Tuesday   7

Wednesday   8

Thursday   9

Friday 10

Saturday 11

Sunday 12

JANUARY 2025

Week 3

Monday **13**

Tuesday **14**

Wednesday **15**

Thursday **16**

Friday 17

Saturday 18

Sunday 19

JANUARY 2025

Week 4

Monday **20**

Tuesday **21**

Wednesday **22**

Thursday **23**

Friday 24

Saturday 25

Sunday 26

JANUARY 2025

Week 5

Monday 27

Tuesday 28

Wednesday 29

Thursday 30

Friday 31

FEBRUARY 2025

Saturday 1

Sunday 2

FEBRUARY 2025

Week 6

Monday   3

Tuesday   4

Wednesday   5

Thursday   6

Friday   **7**

Saturday   **8**

Sunday   **9**

FEBRUARY 2025

Week 7

Monday　　10

Tuesday　　11

Wednesday　12

Thursday　　13

Friday   **14**   *Valentine's Day*

Saturday   **15**

Sunday   **16**

FEBRUARY 2025

Week 8

Monday   17

Tuesday   18

Wednesday 19

Thursday   20

Friday 21

Saturday 22

Sunday 23

FEBRUARY 2025

Week 9

Monday   24

Tuesday   25

Wednesday 26

Thursday   27

Friday   28

MARCH 2025

Saturday   1   *St David's Day*

Sunday   2

MARCH 2025

Week 10

Monday   3 _____

Tuesday   4 _____

Wednesday   5 _____

Thursday   6 _____

Friday 7

Saturday 8

Sunday 9

MARCH 2025

Week 11

Monday   10

Tuesday   11

Wednesday 12

Thursday   13

Friday   **14**

Saturday   **15**

Sunday   **16**

MARCH 2025

Week 12

| Monday | 17 | *St Patrick's Day* |

| Tuesday | 18 |

| Wednesday | 19 |

| Thursday | 20 |

Friday 21

Saturday 22

Sunday 23

MARCH 2025
Week 13

Monday   24

Tuesday   24

Wednesday   26

Thursday   27

Friday   **28**

Saturday   **29**

Sunday   **30**   *UK Mother's Day*

MARCH 2025

Week 14

Monday   31

APRIL 2025

Tuesday   1

Wednesday   2

Thursday   3

Friday   4

Saturday   5

Sunday   6

APRIL 2025

Week 15

Monday 7

Tuesday 8

Wednesday 9

Thursday 10

Friday 11

Saturday 12

Sunday 13

APRIL 2025

Week 16

Monday   14

Tuesday   15

Wednesday 16

Thursday   17

Friday 18   *Good Friday*

Saturday 19

Sunday 20   *Easter Sunday*

APRIL 2025

Week 17

Monday 21   *Easter Monday*

Tuesday 22

Wednesday 23   *St George's Day*

Thursday 24

Friday   25

Saturday   26

Sunday   27

APRIL 2025
Week 18

Monday   28

Tuesday   29

Wednesday 30

MAY 2025

Thursday 1

Friday 2

Saturday 3

Sunday 4

MAY 2025
Week 19

Monday 5 | *Early May Bank Holiday*

Tuesday 6

Wednesday 7

Thursday 8

Friday 9

Saturday 10

Sunday 11

MAY 2025

Week 20

Monday 12

Tuesday 13

Wednesday 14

Thursday 15

Friday   16

Saturday   17

Sunday   18

MAY 2025

Week 21

Monday   19

Tuesday   20

Wednesday   21

Thursday   22

Friday   **23**

Saturday   **24**

Sunday   **25**

MAY 2025

Week 22

Monday	26	*Spring Bank Holiday*

Tuesday	27

Wednesday	28

Thursday	29

Friday 30

Saturday 31

JUNE 2025

Sunday 1

JUNE 2025

Week 23

Monday   2

Tuesday   3

Wednesday   4

Thursday   5

Friday 6

Saturday 7

Sunday 8

JUNE 2025

Week 24

Monday   9

Tuesday   10

Wednesday 11

Thursday   12

Friday 13

Saturday 14

Sunday 15   *UK Father's Day*

JUNE 2025

Week 25

Monday   16

Tuesday   17

Wednesday   18

Thursday   19

Friday   **20**

Saturday   **21**   *King's Birthday*

Sunday   **22**

JUNE 2025

Week 26

Monday   23

Tuesday   24

Wednesday 25

Thursday   26

Friday   **27**

Saturday   **28**

Sunday   **29**

JUNE 2025

Week 27

Monday   30

JULY 2025

Tuesday   1

Wednesday   2

Thursday   3

Friday 4

Saturday 5

Sunday 6

JULY 2025

Week 28

Monday 7

Tuesday 8

Wednesday 9

Thursday 10

Friday 11

Saturday 12

Sunday 13

JULY 2025
Week 29

Monday   14

Tuesday   15

Wednesday 16

Thursday   17

Friday 18

Saturday 19

Sunday 20

JULY 2025

Week 30

Monday 21

Tuesday 22

Wednesday 23

Thursday 24

Friday 25

Saturday 26

Sunday 27

JULY 2025

Week 31

Monday 28

Tuesday 29

Wednesday 30

Thursday 31

AUGUST 2025

Friday   1

Saturday   2

Sunday   3

AUGUST 2025

Week 32

Monday   4

Tuesday   5

Wednesday   6

Thursday   7

Friday 8

Saturday 9

Sunday 10

AUGUST 2025

Week 33

Monday   11

Tuesday   12

Wednesday 13

Thursday   14

Friday   **15**

Saturday   **16**

Sunday   **17**

AUGUST 2025

Week 34

Monday   18

Tuesday   19

Wednesday 20

Thursday   21

Friday   22

Saturday   23

Sunday   24

AUGUST 2025

Week 35

Monday   25   *Summer Bank Holiday*

Tuesday   26

Wednesday 27

Thursday   28

Friday   29

Saturday   30

Sunday   31

SEPTEMBER 2025

Week 36

Monday   **1**

Tuesday   **2**

Wednesday   **3**

Thursday   **4**

Friday   **5**

Saturday   **6**

Sunday   **7**

SEPTEMBER 2025

Week 37

Monday   **8**

Tuesday   **9**

Wednesday 10

Thursday   **11**

Friday   **12**

Saturday   **13**

Sunday   **14**

SEPTEMBER 2025

Week 38

Monday   15

Tuesday   16

Wednesday 17

Thursday   18

Friday 19

Saturday 20

Sunday 21

SEPTEMBER 2025

Week 39

Monday   22

Tuesday   23

Wednesday 24

Thursday   25

Friday   **26**

Saturday   **27**

Sunday   **28**

SEPTEMBER 2025

Week 40

Monday 29

Tuesday 30

OCTOBER 2025

Wednesday 1

Thursday 2

Friday 3

Saturday 4

Sunday 5

OCTOBER 2025

Week 41

Monday   6

Tuesday   7

Wednesday   8

Thursday   9

Friday 10

Saturday 11

Sunday 12

OCTOBER 2025

Week 42

Monday 13

Tuesday 14

Wednesday 15

Thursday 16

Friday 17

Saturday 18

Sunday 19

OCTOBER 2025

Week 43

Monday   20

Tuesday   21

Wednesday 22

Thursday   23

Friday   **24**

Saturday   **25**

Sunday   **26**

OCTOBER 2025

Week 44

Monday   27

Tuesday   28

Wednesday 29

Thursday 30

Friday 31 *Halloween*

NOVEMBER 2025

Saturday 1

Sunday 2

NOVEMBER 2025

Week 45

Monday   3

Tuesday   4

Wednesday   5   *Guy Fawkes Day*

Thursday   6

Friday 7

Saturday 8

Sunday 9 *Remembrance Sunday*

NOVEMBER 2025

Week 46

Monday   10

Tuesday   11

Wednesday 12

Thursday   13

Friday   **14**

Saturday   **15**

Sunday   **16**

NOVEMBER 2025

Week 47

Monday 17

Tuesday 18

Wednesday 19

Thursday 20

Friday   **21**

Saturday   **22**

Sunday   **23**

NOVEMBER 2025

Week 48

Monday   24

Tuesday   25

Wednesday   26

Thursday   27

Friday 28

Saturday 29

Sunday 30   *St Andrew's Day*

DECEMBER 2025

Week 49

Monday   1

Tuesday   2

Wednesday   3

Thursday   4

Friday   **5**

Saturday   **6**

Sunday   **7**

DECEMBER 2025

Week 50

Monday   **8**

Tuesday   **9**

Wednesday 10

Thursday   **11**

Friday   **12**

Saturday   **13**

Sunday   **14**

DECEMBER 2025

Week 51

Monday   15

Tuesday   16

Wednesday   17

Thursday   18

Friday 19

Saturday 20

Sunday 21

DECEMBER 2025

Week 52

Monday 22

Tuesday 23

Wednesday 24 *Christmas Eve*

Thursday 25 *Christmas Day*

Friday 26   *Boxing Day*

Saturday 27

Sunday 28

DECEMBER 2025

Week 1

Monday   29

Tuesday   30

Wednesday 31   *New Year's Eve*

JANUARY 2026

Thursday   1   *New Year's Day*

Friday   2

Saturday   3

Sunday   4

NOTES

NOTES

Printed in Great Britain
by Amazon

50883612R00066